GOLD

The Poiema Poetry Series

Poems are windows into worlds; windows into beauty, goodness, and truth; windows into understandings that won't twist themselves into tidy dogmatic statements; windows into experiences. We can do more than merely peer into such windows; with a little effort we can fling open the casements, and leap over the sills into the heart of these worlds. We are also led into familiar places of hurt, confusion, and disappointment, but we arrive in the poet's company. Poetry is a partnership between poet and reader, seeking together to gain something of value—to get at something important.

Ephesians 2:10 says, "We are God's workmanship . . ." *poiema* in Greek— the thing that has been made, the masterpiece, the poem. The Poiema Poetry Series presents the work of gifted poets who take Christian faith seriously, and demonstrate in whose image we have been made through their creativity and craftsmanship.

These poets are recent participants in the ancient tradition of David, Asaph, Isaiah, and John the Revelator. The thread can be followed through the centuries—through the diverse poetic visions of Dante, Bernard of Clairvaux, Donne, Herbert, Milton, Hopkins, Eliot, R.S. Thomas, and Denise Levertov—down to the poet whose work is in your hand. With the selection of this volume you are entering this enduring tradition, and as a reader contributing to it.

—D.S. Martin
Series Editor

Collections in this series include:
Six Sundays toward a Seventh by Sydney Lea
Epitaphs for the Journey by Paul Mariani
Within This Tree of Bones by Robert Siegel
Particular Scandals by Julie L. Moore
A Word In My Mouth by Robert Cording (*forthcoming*)

Gold

BARBARA CROOKER

CASCADE *Books* • Eugene, Oregon

GOLD

Cascade Books
An Imprint of Wipf and Stock Publishers
199 W. 8th Ave., Suite 3
Eugene, OR 97401

www.wipfandstock.com

ISBN 13: 978-1-62032-940-5

Cataloging-in-Publication data:

Crooker, Barbara, 1945–.

Gold / Barbara Crooker.

x + 70 p.; 23 cm

ISBN 13: 978-1-62032-940-5

1. American poetry—21st century. I. Title. II. Series.

PS3553 .R548 G35 2013

Manufactured in the USA.

Acknowledgments

Adanna: "First Spring Without You"

Appalachee Review: "Rendezvous at Annecy"

Ardent: "Distance"

Calyx: "Weather Report"

Canary: "Late August"

Christianity & Literature: "In Praise of Dying"

Crannóg (Ireland): "Leaf Light"

The Cresset: "Plenitude," "Late Prayer," "God's Tears"

Dogwood: "On the Day of Her Diagnosis"

Earth's Daughters: "Sparklers"

Earthspeak: "Variations on a Line by my Daughter at Three"

5 AM: "Salt"

Gargoyle: "All Saints," "Very Long Afternoons"

Hospital Drive: "Soft"

The Innisfree Poetry Journal: "Worlds End," "The Last Painting"

Iodine: "Zucchini"

The Journal of New Jersey Poets: "The Burren"

Kansas City Voices: "Invoice"

Louisiana Literature: "Ecdysiast"

The Mom Egg: "Manet and the Sea"

Off the Coast: "La neige et l'hiver"

Perspectives: "Gold"

Poet Lore: "Sugar"

qarrtsiluni: "1950"

Relief: "Peeps," "Aubade"

Rock & Sling: "Judas Tree"

Ruminate: "June," "Pistachios"

St. Katherine Review: "At VCCA, I Hear a Red-Bellied Woodpecker, and
   Think of Martha Silano,"

Simul: "Snippet"

South Carolina Review: "Ashes," "The Table my Mother's Brother Kept,"

Spillway: "Willow Ware"

Acknowledgments

String Poet: "Today," "A Woman Is her Mother. That's the Main Thing."
   "Grief," "Siberian Iris"
Switched-On Gutenberg: "The Stock Market Loses Fluidity"
Tar River Review: "Owl Hour"
Tiferet: "Vaudeville"
Triplopia: "My Mother's Body Knits Itself into a Nest of Pain,"
The Valparaiso Poetry Review: "Oriental Poppies"
Verse Wisconsin: "Mother," "Goddesses," "Stones"
Wisconsin Review: "Ambrosia"

"Owl Hour, "Sugar," and "La neige et l'hiver" also appeared in *Fire on Her Tongue: An e-book Anthology of Contemporary Women's Poetry* (Two Sylvias Press). "The Burren" was a finalist for the 2011 New Jersey Poets' Prize. "Ecdysiast" was selected for a juried reading and art/photography exhibit, "Living Among Giants: Seeing the Forest for the Trees," at the D&R Greenway Foundation. "A Woman Is her Mother. That's the Main Thing." received Honorable Mention and "Today," was a finalist in 2011 String Poet Prize competition. "Invoice" and "A Woman Is her Mother. That's the Main Thing." were nominated for a 2011 Pushcart Prize. "Oriental Poppies" was nominated for a 2011 Best of the Net Award. "On the Day of Her Diagnosis" was selected for the "Voices on Motherhood" exhibition of the International Museum of Women, and received Honorable Mention and publication in *The Cancer Poetry Project II* (Working Words). It also appeared in *Quill and Parchment, Kaleidoscope,* and on *Poet's Corner.* "Siberian Iris" also appeared on mugs in the Coffee Cup Poetry Project. "The Stock Market Loses Fluidity" and "Zucchini" also appeared on *Your Daily Poem.* "Leaf Light" also appeared on *Poet's Corner,* as did "Worlds End." "Ashes" also appeared on *Poetry Life and Times.* "Mother" also appeared in *Kaleidoscope.* "Deauville: Le Paddock" and "Rendezvous at Annency" were part of the Look of Love exhibit in Barrington, IL. "Stones" and "God's Tears" were part of the Handprint Identity Project, an ekphrastic exhibit and pamphlet.

Many thanks to the Virginia Center for the Creative Arts and the Jesuit Center, Wernersville, PA for the gift of space and silence, to my friends in writing, Ken Fifer, Marjorie Stelmach, Barbara Reisner, Kathy Moser, and Geri Rosenzweig, who looked at many of the poems in this manuscript;

Gray Jacobik, for her excellent advice; my husband, Dick; my children, Stacey, Rebecca, David; and my grandchildren, Daniel and Caitlin; and, of course, my mother, Isabelle Charlotte Smith Poti.

Nothing gold can stay.
—ROBERT FROST

Table of Contents

Table of Contents

one

Invoice

The moon lays down white covers on the bed,
some small hedge against the long night.
A great horned owl's call sends dread

up and down small spines. Turn out the light,
pull up the wool blanket, shut the window,
because one day too soon I'll sleep alone. Tonight,

the moon's a sliver of lemon in a cup of espresso,
and I'm too jittery to sleep. I count my breaths,
their rise and fall, by the alarm clock's digital glow,

an unearthly green. Soon dawn will spread
a smear of pink on the horizon, and another golden
October day begins. Sometimes, there's so much death—

the year, the leaves, old friends—it's hard to hold on
to what anchors us to everyday stuff:
coffee in a mug, buttered toast, the same old sun

returning. Some days, it's hard to see beneath
the surface. Three white butterflies weave, twine
the air around the Russian sage, late roses, enough,

enough. The nasturtiums, red, gold, orange, unwind,
green hand over hand, turn the cement stoop
into a little bit of Ireland. What shines

will not be forgotten. Is this how a scoop
of brandy would sound, if it had a voice?
The sky flings out its bolt of cotton, that hue

of blue cerulean. What choice
when the world burns to ash, to gold?

Vaudeville

Late October, and the sky is that clear blue scrim
we only see when the leaves go presto chango, garnet
and gold, and asters and chrysanthemums, the last
flowers, take their bow on center stage. The birds
are packing it up, preparing their exit, and the rest
of the garden collapses in ruin: fallen branches,
crumpled programs, dried leaves. The house light
turns everything golden, and even though we know
what's coming, the next act, we start to believe
we can stay here forever in the amber spotlight,
that night's black velvet curtain will never fall.

Ecdysiast

This maple tree's slipped into something
scarlet, which she'll peel off slowly,
leaf by leaf. Look at her showing
her bare limbs and bark. She knows
that age is just another ring, a thing
she's happy to accumulate. O tree,
your buds are in the bank, already
deposited in the securities
of twig and branch. Your red silk
slip, gorgeous on these sheets
of satin blue, will fray and crumple,
turn into rags. Sooner, or later,
we'll all fall down.

Gold

The goldenrod's tarnished and dull, gone to rust,
as the Dow Jones plummets like the mercury
on a January night, echoing Frost's warning
that *nothing gold can stay.* Not the birch
leaves that glittered like sequins on a tap
line, not the marigold's petals, not the finch's
wing. It falls through our fingers, pebbles
in a placer's pan. We try to spend it,
but the days are too short, and the stores
won't give us credit. We try to bank it,
but our password is denied. When the clocks
give back their hour, when at dinnertime it's dark
as a politician's heart, where do those minutes go?
Do they jangle their golden music as they slip
through the holes in our linty pockets
to fall on the frozen hard ground?

The Stock Market Loses Fluidity

2008 NPR headline

I'll show you what's *really* liquid—it's this sunlight
pouring down from the west, from the great glass jar
of the sky. The creek playing its little tune, running
over the stones. The descant of syllables
in the mockingbird's song. For not a single
hickory nut banked by the squirrels will gain
any interest. Not a grain of wheat in the wallet
of a chipmunk's cheek will increase in worth.
The bear's fat layer is its IRA. Here in the woods,
it's autumn's great investment portfolio; look,
everything's turned the color of money:
copper, brass, gold.

Leaf Light

Leaf by leaf, the trees let down their gold;
everything returns to dirt: stem,
bark, twig. The corn stalks have dried
to papery whispers, speak a new language
in the wind's harsh breath. It's October, when
leaf means *loss*, and bird means *go*. Today,
the grass glitters greenly, freshened by last week's
rain, and fallen apples, red and yellow, dot
the lawn. You and I are trying to get a fire
going again; we crumple up papers, snap twigs
for kindling, haul in logs from the wood pile.
Sparks fly up the chimney. Everything burns.

Variations on a Line by my Daughter at Three

I not was doing nothing. Becky Crooker

Fat yellow leaves pile
against a white picket fence,
and the sugar maples let go,
showers of sparks from a bonfire.
They will rise again in braids of smoke.
Geese blare discordant chords, fall
into formation; starlings gather
on telephone wires. This is migration's
long dance. At twilight, deer tiptoe
down the path to nibble windfalls.
There's Showy Goldenrod, there's
Pearly Everlasting, there's Late Purple Aster,
and Joe-Pye Weed. Now, night falls early,
covers us with its bowl of stars. And there is
not one bit of this that is not beautiful.

Late Prayer

It's not that I'm not trying
to love the world and everything
in it, but look, that includes people
who shoot up schools, not just the blue
bird in his coat of sky, his red & white vest,
or the starry asters speckling the field—
It has to include talk show hosts
and all their blather, men with closed
minds and hard hearts, not only this sky,
full of clouds as a field of sheep,
or this wind, pregnant with rain. Don't
I have enough in my life; what is this
wild longing? Is there more to this world
than the shining surfaces? Will I be strong
enough to row across the ocean of loss
when my turn comes to take the oars?

Plenitude

Late fall, but the sun's still warm, streams
in from the west like honey. My hands curl
around a mug of tea, and it feels like a benediction,
a reprieve from my crazy life: bringing my mother
from one doctor to the other, as systems shut down,
doors start to close; going to interviews
with my disabled son to find, in the end,
that promised programs aren't funded,
and when school ends in June, that's it, so long.
But today, there's this—the happiness that comes
from working again, even though rejections
fill my mailbox, thicker than snowflakes.
I know winter's waiting; I've felt its breath
on the back of the wind. This is a bit of respite
before the storms roll in. I lean against this willow,
let the sun soak all the way to the bones. These blue
mountains cup me in their hands. This lucent afternoon
and a spigot of birdsong fill my bowl to the brim.

All Saints

It's one day past the Day of the Dead, and this has been
a bad year, six funerals already and not done yet.
But on this blue day of perfect weather, I can't muster
sadness, for the trees are radiant, the air thick as Karo
warmed in a pan. I have my friend's last book spread
on the table and a cup of coffee in a white china mug.
All the leaves are ringing, like the tiny bells of God.
My mother, too, is ready to leave. All she wants now
is sugar: penuche fudge, tapioca pudding, pumpkin roll.
She wants to sit in the sun, pull it around her shoulders
like an Orlon sweater, and listen to the birds
in the far-off trees. I want this sweetness to linger
on her tongue, because the days are growing shorter
now, and night comes on, so quickly.

My Mother's Body Knits Itself Into a Nest of Pain,

bones milling themselves into flour.
No escape, not sitting in the chair
with cushions, not lying in bed
wrapped in night's black afghan,
but pain as a constant, the one X
equals in every equation.

No honey is sweet enough
for this dark cup of tea.
I bake her favorite shortbread,
make peanut butter fudge,
bring her dinner in a wicker basket,
like Red Riding Hood. She doesn't
turn into a wolf, just the ghost of herself,
becoming part of the past while she's still
here. I might as well carry sugar in my hands;
grain by grain, she sifts away.

On the Day of her Diagnosis

a cold wind was bearing
down, straight from Canada.

The small pearl I'd seen floating
in the warm water of her breast

was cancer, a word that hissed
in the ear like fat in a pan

or the breath of a snake.
With these two syllables, the dice

rolled, and the odds went down
for all the women in my family.

Early November, most of October's
gold has fallen, bruise-colored clouds

moving in. I remember being six,
sick in bed, how the winter trees

scratched the leaden sky, witches in a Grimm
tale, how she brought me cinnamon

toast and milky tea. Now I bring her lentil
soup, with circles of kielbasa, carrots, onions;

scones warm from the oven, spread with strawberry
jam, whatever bit of sweetness I can scrape

from the jar. Mother, daughter, all the old stories,
the frost moon, the loss moon, sinking below the horizon.

Worlds End

We were sitting on the rocks, my husband
and son, down by the Loyalsock Creek,

in a stone cabin built by the CCC. Back
home, my mother cannot sleep—her recliner's

too small, the hospital bed's too hard—
like Goldilocks in the bears' cottage,

nothing is just right. Nothing will ever be
just right, as her body fails and fails

some more. Up on a ridge above the Loyalsock,
the trees are at their peak. Even the creek water

burns red, orange, yellow. The cell phone
in my pocket in case hospice calls thumps

against my thigh. It's one of those brilliant
blue days you think should last forever,

the trees glowing redder, starry asters
lining the rocky path. Back in the cabin,

pork and cranberries have been slowly cooking all day.
I boil wild rice, add toasted pine nuts, yellow raisins.

At home, my mother lifts a bowl, fills her nebulizer,
inhales the hot steam, breathes more easily for a little

while. I throw more wood in the black iron stove,
whose hunger is insatiable, whose belly can never be filled.

two

Ambrosia

Whenever I brought her something she'd liked,
my mother would say, *Ambrosia. That's what this is,*
pure ambrosia. It might have been complicated, chicken
in basil cream with Sauvignon Blanc on fresh linguine.
Or a dense chocolate cake, sour cream and hot coffee
in the batter. But often, it was simple, a sun-warm
tomato or peach. At the end, when she weighed
eighty-five pounds and wouldn't eat the bland food
on her tray, what she wanted, above all else,
was donuts: marble-swirled, sugar-powdered,
honey-glazed, thickly iced with neon sprinkles, filled
with the jeweled ooze of jelly. . . . And best of all,
Boston Creme, pale memory of her favorite birthday cake.
Right hand limp under the sheet, she grabbed that donut
in her left, and squeezed. The pallid yellow filling
ran down her arm, and chocolate oozed between her fingers.
When the chewy dough was gone, she licked the rest off,
every bit. And when she was done, she sighed. *Ambrosia.*

June

The treacle of birdsong pours over our heads,
and the afternoon drowses in the heat. Only
the butterflies are industrious, skipping
from the foxgloves to roses the color
of old bricks. Even in her wheelchair,
my mother is still surprised
when she sees a pink water lily
rising out of the mud. When I push her
past it on the way back, she gets surprised
all over again. I pick her a dandelion;
it smells of nothing but summer. Later,
when it goes to seed, we will make a wish
before our breath sends its parachutes
spinning across the lawn. I think about
her last mammogram, the clusters of nebulae,
and the black hole where cancer's random
toss planted its seed. Out in the grass,
the dandelions spread their thin spatulate
leaves, dig their tough roots
deeper, ready for any weather.

Snippet

That mockingbird's going jabber, jabber, jabber;
doesn't he ever shut up? Early June, and the peonies
have finally opened; they nod their pink heads
in the soft sweet wind. The afternoon begins
to blossom, the air like table syrup, the lawn,
a bowl of sunshine. From far off, a woodpecker
is knocking, knocking. Batter my heart, three-
personed God, dip it in flour, salt, and milk;
fry it up, good and golden as this afternoon,
one shining lake of light.

Late August

So already, everything's starting to turn,
grackles crocheting their raggedy
scarves as they fly from the woods, snap beans
rusting and brown, tomatoes still pulsing
yellow stars in the hope that they'll swell
round and red before frost shuts down
their production lines. Right now, we can still
dry them in the sun, pack them in oil, or slowly
roast them with garlic and thyme.
But nothing beats this sweetness in August,
hot and heavy with juice and seeds. Slice
them into rounds, shuffle with mozzarella,
add basil's anise nip, drizzle with the kiss
of *olio di oliva*, a dark splash of balsamic,
the sprinkled grit of sea salt. The circles ring the plate,
diminishing O's. We know the party's almost over,
the sun's packing its bags. Listen to the crows
outside the cold window: *gone gone gone.*

In Praise of Dying

after a poem by Sue Ellen Thompson

For giving us these last six weeks
where we reversed, and I read to her,
a novel about Africa, where neither of us

has ever been. For letting that novel
remind her how much she loved donuts,
their greasy faces shining through brown

paper bags. For Dunkin' Donuts,
their many glazed varieties.
For the afternoons that weren't too hot,

weren't too humid, that let me push her
in the wheelchair to see the koi flashing in
and out of the water lilies. For letting me be

her legs. When the end came, for letting me
slip some soup into her parched mouth,
rub cream on her hands and feet,

place a sweater around her shoulders,
all bone now. Watch her breathe
in the night, like she watched me

when I was new. For letting her
go out as quietly as a candle
that has used up all its wax.

For letting me be there
for her last breath
that fluttered out like a moth.

Peeps

In those last few months my mother didn't want to eat,
this woman who made everything from scratch,
and who said of her appetite, *I eat like a bricklayer.*
Now she listlessly stirred the food around her plate,
sometimes picking up a piece of chicken,
then looking at it as if to say, *What is this?* Wouldn't
put it in her mouth. But Peeps! Marshmallow Peeps!
Spun sugar and air, molded in clever forms: a row
of ghosts, a line of pumpkins, a bevy of bunnies,
a flock of tiny chicks, sometimes in improbable colors
like purple and blue. . . . One day, she turned over
her tray, closed her mouth, looked up at me
like a defiant child, and said, *I'm not eating this stuff.*
Where's my Peeps?

When it was over, the hospice chaplain said some words
in my back yard, under the wisteria arch. The air was full
of twinkling white butterflies, in love with the wild
oregano. Blue-green fronds of Russian sage waved
in front of the Star Gazer lilies, and a single finch
lit on a pink coneflower, and stayed. When there were
no more words or tears, I ripped open the last packet
of Peeps, tore their little marshmallow bodies,
their sugary blood on my hands, and gave a piece
to each of us. It melted, grainy fluff
on our tongues, and it was good.

Oriental Poppies

after a painting by Georgia O'Keeffe: "Oriental Poppies, 1928"

Lit matches struck in the dark, road-flares
burning, these poppies smolder by the bird bath
where we cradled my mother's ashes
when her life wicked out. Each flower
is splotched with black, night at the heart
of burning day. Light shines through the petals,
translucent as skin. At the end, her bones shone through,
the skeleton wanting to dance. The poppies' orange tango,
a wild fandango with the wind. Nothing in English rhymes
with this color, not porridge, not ordinary, not original.
We only have one mother. Reach for a blossom,
twirl it in your fingers, a dancer on an unlit stage.
Every gardener knows about loss: thinning, pruning,
the appetite of rabbits, how frost waits in the wings,
sharpening his shears.

Ashes

Later, we brought her ashes to the beach
at the end of Pilgrim Road, and I poured them out
as fast as I could, standing knee-deep
in the seaweedy shallows, because it had started
to rain, and I didn't want her to get wet.
What was I thinking? She was returning
to our first mother, the sea. But all I wanted
to do was gather up every gritty particle,
every chip of bone, then mix them with my bare
hands, using sand and mud, saliva and tears,
and bring her back, my own personal golem.
How could I have let her sift out of my fingers,
grain by grain? The heavier bits sank, mixed
with broken shells; the lighter ones blew
in the wind, stuck to the patches of foam.
How can she be gone?

La neige et l'hiver

after a study in acrylic, ink, & encaustic by Claire Giblin

I stretch my canvas tight as a sail,
size it with gesso, sand it down,
apply layers of oils, wave
after wave of powdered
pigment, beeswax, melt them
with a torch. I'm trying to fix
the fog's sfumato as it speaks
in the old mother tongue:
horizon   cloud   sea.

***

Light, both particle and wave,
is the dark ground I'm working on,
the gouache of my mother's death.
An empty beach after the tide recedes:
ribbed sand, striations of clouds.

***

The seasons change, peel off their coats.
Grief comes and goes with its shaker of salt,
pours over me without warning. Puts items
in my grocery cart that only she would eat.

***

Everything is blurred, time folding back
on itself. My palette's a smudgy grisaille
of slate, steel, smoke. And ochre.

***

It was like morning on the first day
when she passed, land dividing
from sea, air from water, soul
from body. What remained
was a coracle, a small boat
with a canvas for its sail.

Mother

Mid-October, and the sky is a heartless, relentless blue.
Every day, the sycamores turn a little more golden,
as if the sky is a celestial toaster turned up high,
and I'm waiting for it to ding. I am wishing
my mother could come back, or send me a sign.
Is she the goldfinch at the thistle feeder, shrugged
into an olive drab cardigan? Or the monarch

hinging and unhinging her stained-glass wings
as she lights on the chrysanthemums one more time
before she leaves for Mexico? Are there birds
where you are, Mother? Do you miss the sun?
You have been gone three months now,
a quarter of a year. It feels like three minutes;
it feels like forever. You have missed

this fall, this blaze of glory. Yesterday, I made
that chicken dish you loved, the one with olives
and garlic bobbing like small boats
in the wine-dark sea. I fried up polenta,
sliced it in golden circles. The woven picnic
basket where I'd put your foil-covered plate
is empty. So is my heart.

Grief

is a river you wade in until you get to the other side.
But I am here, stuck in the middle, water parting
around my ankles, moving downstream
over the flat rocks. I'm not able to lift a foot,
move on. Instead, I'm going to stay here
in the shallows with my sorrow, nurture it
like a cranky baby, rock it in my arms.
I don't want it to grow up, go to school, get married.
It's mine. Yes, the October sunlight wraps me
in its yellow shawl, and the air is sweet
as a golden Tokay. On the other side,
there are apples, grapes, walnuts,
and the rocks are warm from the sun.
But I'm going to stand here,
growing colder, until every inch
of my skin is numb. I can't cross over.
Then you really will be gone.

First Spring Without You

Then you'll remember your life
as a book of candles,
each page read
by the light of its burning.
("Become Becoming," Li-Young Lee)

I'm driving south, spring unrolling like a satin
ribbon right off the spool. Trees blur with the whisper
of buds, fresh green hope. You've gone to the place
of no return, and that's the black branched fact. Along
the highway, impossibly purple redbuds arc overhead,
and I want to pull over, take pictures to show you
when I return. Time keeps zigzagging, past/present/past,
like that fat red fox running in the meadow's tall grass.
The trees' blossoms are incandescent as candles,
but the Book of Life is fastened shut,
and there are no pages left to read by their own burning.

Goddesses

We were in the National Museum of Women in the Arts,
looking at dresses by Mary McFadden, our English Major
minds thinking of goddesses like Aphrodite, Venus,
Jackie Kennedy, their pleated tunics, their embroidered
and beaded gowns. We were talking about Enheduanna,
the first poet, and what her words mean now, coming down
through the fabric of time. But what was on our hearts,
here in the Capitol, where men make monuments
of cold white stones, was our mothers, both recently gone.
Their absence, an old one, Persephone and Demeter
in reverse, winter's frozen length of shot-silk, spring's
return in green brocade. But there is no returning
in this story, each of us unmothered now. Grief
has dressed us in black caftans. Across town,
in the Tidal Basin, the Yoshino cherry trees
have let down their gorgeous petals, wrapping
the earth in pink ribbons, the way a ballerina tapes
her ankles in silk that seems fragile, but is strong
enough to keep her on her toes
as long as she needs to remain *en pointe.*

Today,

the sky's a flawless blue, as if someone from Sherman
Williams had dumped a bucket of Dazzle (#6962)
over the naked clear dome. That blue. The maples
let go their seeds, samaras whirlygigging in the breeze.
One more letter, and it's *samsara,* the Sanskrit word
for the cycle of birth, suffering, death, rebirth.
I hear the 4:45 to Lynchburg rumble under the trestle
cut in the kudzu-covered hillside, its whistle
the lonesomest sound around. *Sometimes,*
I feel like a motherless child, and now I am.
The sky is heartless as well as cloudless.
I turn and look, but she's not there.

A Woman Is her Mother. That's the Main Thing.

A woman is her mother, that's the only thing.
After the first death, there is no other.
It's April, and loss is in the air.
Trees lose their blossoms in this weather.

After the first death, no other
grief matters. April, loss everywhere,
trees let their blossoms fall.
I want you back, I want you here,

even though April's loss brings on the flowers,
trees forming new buds along each branch.
But there's no turning back for us,
whose calyx, pistil, ovary blooms in flesh.

And each tree has a different seed: wings, pods, cones.
It's an old story, . . .replacement, a way back
as a grandchild wears your eyes, your chin, your mouth.
But it's not you, to whom I need to talk.

The only way back is to go forward.
It's April, grief everywhere.
I want to call you on the telephone.
A woman *is* her mother, but alone.

The Table my Mother's Brother Kept,

though it was promised to her,
was made by their father at his lumber

yard, the one he owned, then lost
in the Great Depression, where he

had to go back to work as an hourly
employee. It was a small table, not

useful except as a plant stand,
with thin drawers, carefully joined.

She wanted it because his hands
had turned the legs, glued the boards,

sanded them smooth, applied
the stain, brought out the grain,

rubbed it to a luster with butcher's
wax. She wanted it not for its beauty,

but because it was a letter,
from father to daughter.

Because nothing remained
of the house on King Philip Road

except this piece of furniture.
Not veneer but some hardwood,

walnut or mahogany, mortised
with a carpenter's square and aligned

with a spirit-level, so that each drawer
in its slot slid home plumb and true.

three

Sparklers

We're writing our names with sizzles of light
to celebrate the fourth. I use the loops of cursive,
make a big *B* like the sloping hills on the west side
of the lake. The rest, little *a*, *r*, one small *b*,
spit and fizz as they scratch the night. On the side
of the shack where we bought them, a handmade sign:
Trailer Full of Sparkles Ahead, and I imagine crazy
chrysanthemums, wheels of fire, glitter bouncing
off metal walls. Here, we keep tracing in tiny
pyrotechnics the letters we were given at birth,
branding them on the air. And though my mother's
name has been erased now, I write it, too:
a big swooping *I*, a little hissing *s*, an *a* that sighs
like her last breath, and then I ring
belle, belle, belle in the sulphuric smoky dark.

Monopoly: 1955

We start by fanning out the money, colored
like Necco wafers: pink, yellow, mint, gold.
From the first roll of the dice, differences widen:
the royal blues of Boardwalk and Park Place
look down their noses at the grapey immigrants
from Baltic and Mediterranean Avenues.
My grandparents coming from Italy in steerage
measured their gold in olive oil, not bank notes
and deeds. The man in the top hat and tuxedo
always holds the good cards. The rest of us
hope we can pay the Electric Company.
We know there is no such thing as Free Parking,
and Bank Errors are never in our favor.
In the background, Johnny Mathis croons
Chances Are from the cracked vinyl radio.
We played for hours, in those years
before television, on the Formica table,
while my mother coaxed a chicken,
cooking all day on the back burner, to multiply
itself into many meals. The fat rose to the surface,
a roiling ocean of molten gold.

1950

When it was still safe to walk home alone—scuffling
in leaves, which people burned at the curb—we skipped
from the brick schoolhouse to the brown-shingled
Village Hall where we did good deeds, earned
embroidered badges. Our mothers' lives
were sewn up tight, constricted by lack of cars,
highlighted by the bing bong of the Avon lady,
her purse full of samples; the Fuller Brush man,
his valise that unfolded in triple layers;
or, down the street, the squeaky brakes
of the Peter Wheat Bread truck. Oh, the thick
icing on those cupcakes, the ligature
of the white squiggle. Which my mother rarely
bought. How we long for what we cannot have.
How it all goes up in smoke.

The Last Painting

Arshile Gorky Retrospective,
Philadelphia Museum of Art

I'd always seen his name wrong, Ashile, not Arshile,
missed the *r* completely, didn't see the demarcation
of its black arc breaking up the greasy softness
of *ah* and *sh*. I didn't know about the studio fire
that destroyed ten years' work, the cancer
that smoldered in his gut, the marriage
that went up in flames. So he did a painting
called *Agony*, reds flickering into browns,
then a series of smudged grisailles:
Charred Beloved. He painted *The Limit*
just before he reached it, took the rope,
its oval mouth like one of his biomorphic
shapes, placed it around his neck, stepped
off the chair. About art, he said,
I don't like the word finish. On the easel,
his *Last Painting* blackly stared.

At the Observatory in Sweet Briar, Under a Field of Stars

We trudge up an unpaved trail until we are on top
of the hill; the road above, the Milky Way, pavéed
with stars. We huddle in the dark, wait to enter
the plastic igloo where the ten inch reflecting
telescope is stored. One by one, we hear God's name
gasped in wonder as we take a peek at Orion's nebula,
the double star of Ursa Major, the hundreds
in Andromeda's cluster, and, then,
there is Saturn, sliced by its ring, quivering
as if suspended on a platinum chain.
We are shrugged into sweaters and scarves,
cold on this April night, peepers singing
down in the swamp many miles away.
And we are dazzled dizzy, stumbling
as we find our way back in the dark,
tired as the light that has fallen on us,
coming from so many light years away.

At VCCA, I Hear a Red-Bellied Woodpecker, and Think of Martha Silano,

because she taught me to connect the synapse
of the gargle of his song to his manifestation
as Bird; contrary to his name, no red on the chest,
just the creamy buff of the underbelly in some
of Turner's oil-lit clouds. The red on his head
bleeds from beak to back, a jaunty cockade;
his back's a Jacob's ladder of black and white,
that old joke about the newspaper.
Do you remember newspapers? They arrived
with the dawn in a thump on your lawn, rolled
in a log, leaking ink that bloomed on your hands.
This morning deliquesces, bleeds newness,
the world becoming itself again, even though
the headlines repeat themselves, and things
are broken that can't be repaired. I want to be
more like the woodpecker, knocking about
his daily business of extracting dinner
from wood, doing carpentry with a beak,
then drumming, drumming for the dumb
fun of making music, the lubadub of sound.
And who, tomorrow morning, will emerge
from his home in a hollow tree,
and knock himself out all over again.

Owl Hour

I don't know why I get so cold at ten o'clock,
but that's when I'm drawn, like some sort
of night bird, to our nest upstairs in the flannel
sheets, once the color of pinot noir, now duller,
patinaed by the silver of our skins. I need to pile
on the blue blanket, the heavy woolen
one from Ireland, the Broken Star quilt,
before I stop shivering. Sometimes the house
itself quivers in the wind. Then you come up,
and we arrange ourselves like a nest
of measuring cups. Some of our friends
now sleep alone, half the set missing.
I've told you *you're not allowed to die first;*
I don't do numbers—checkbook, taxes, bills.
My breasts press into your back; my hand
with the numb fingers stretches
over your heart. How lucky we are
to have found each other; what if
I hadn't gone to the party that night?
The second time for both of us; we know
how it can all go wrong. Even when I can't sleep,
I listen to the hoots and calls of your breathing,
which both keeps me awake and will be
the first thing I'll miss when all the nights
are silent. We know there'll be an *afterwards*;
we're not that young anymore. I turn, and turn
again, the way a dog circles before he lies down.
And though we can't see them, the stars twirl
overhead, each one nested in the place in space
it's supposed to call home.

Soft

I don't want a younger man with a buff body,
a stomach like the washboard my mother
used for laundry after the war. I don't want
to see his hip bones through his taut skin,
the sine curve of his buttocks, the way he doesn't
yet know that sorrow's going to find him. I want
a man with a gut like a chair cushion, something
around the middle to hold on to, sparse silver
hairs springing out of his chest and groin. Under
the chin, ridges and hills slope down to the sea.
My body, too, loosens, sags, the skin letting go,
hair sprouting where I don't want it, but not
where I do. There's sludge in my blood,
crumble in my bones. But under the covers,
in the dark, I can edit him back to the boy
he was, the one I never knew. Our sheets are
flannel, worn thin by erosion. Some nights
we can. Some nights we can't. Let's praise
what's still working. This is every body's story.

Intro to Lit

Coming across my old textbook—cheap paperback,
cracked spine, peeling cover—I leaf through it,
looking for poems. I have no idea my seventeen
year old self is still inside, lounging on the pages
in loopy handwriting I barely recognize as my own,
an odd shade of blue-black ink. . . . Did I check off
Keats's ode *To Autumn* because I liked it, or because
it was required? I hope I loved Auden's *Unknown Citizen*;
I had notes by every line. I wrote at the top of Petronius,
It is in the nature of things to live, to shorten grief.
But what did I know of grieving then, when my heart
was still uncracked? On 325, in someone else's writing,
a note from the girl in the next seat complaining
about her GPA. On 327, she wrote in pencil, *Touch me.*
I'm going to see Bill. Years later, I fell in love
with the Kunitz lines, *Touch me, / remind me who I am*
but neither of us remembers now who Bill was, or what
happened next. We both married early, divorced, married
again. The notes in the margins, hieroglyphics
from a lost age. Where are the boys of yesteryear?

Willow Ware

I was the kind of girl who played alone,
had tea parties under hedges, where
it was dark and cool and my father's
anger couldn't find me, using acorn
caps for plates, moss for a tablecloth,
imagination and air for tea. When no storms
threatened, my mother would let me use
the child-sized blue willow china
her mother had given her, and I would stare
into the small cups, entering the story:
the curved footbridge where a cobalt willow
wept by a tea house with a fancy roof,
two blue swallows winging overhead.
In blue willowland, no fighting
was allowed. Once in a blue moon,
a few clouds floated by. Maybe
we'll all go sailing. *Nel blu dipinto di blu.*

Manet and the Sea

title of an exhibit at the Philadelphia Art Museum

The Escape of Rochfort, 1880–1881
Who cares about those convicts rowing a path
in the moonlight? It's the water we want to look
at, taking its own sweet time as it steps up
to the microphone to solo, an improvisation in blue:

Ohio match tips, mouthwash, flax fields in France.
The moon, once in a while.
The moon, where I saw you standing alone.
The moon, forme d'Ambert, Roquefort, Stilton,
Gorgonzola. Speedwell, rosemary, chicory, plum.
Skies, smiling at me. The wild yonder.
Something to get tangled up in. Twelve bars,
Bessie, Billie, Janis, piano, steel guitars.

Oh, Eddie Manet, he's got the blues,
got paint on his shoes, done paid his dues,
oh, Eddie Manet, he's got the blues,
yeah, he got them blues so bad . . . . .

Siberian Iris

All day long, in the cool grey light of an ice storm,
the tall wands of iris are quietly opening,
first the sepals, then the petals, one
after the other, a striptease in reverse, until
all six of them are fully open, their tongues
hanging out. They are every blue Monday,
they are the House of Blue Light, where
someone is singing something about longing,
someone is singing about the rain.

Distance

And now, there is a space
between us, some blue distance,
and I had to get away,
so I went east to the beach
for a week, where the ocean
was washing its silver change,
and the grasses turned bronze
in the late autumn sun.

Small birds reeled in and out
of the holly, bayberries, scrub oak,
and the clouds whipped themselves up
into a froth of chrysanthemums,
petals shearing off in the wind.

The space between us blossomed
in the afternoon's long light.

A fisherman
casts in the surf,
one more time,
a long silky filament,
the thread that still
joins me to you;
it snaps taut, then loosens,
and he pulls it back in.

four

Sugar

My mother is a hungry ghost. She comes to me
in dreams, asking, *Where's the applesauce?*
The kind you make? Cooked with the skins on,
whirled with cinnamon and nutmeg, swirled
through a food mill, smooth fruit separated
from skins, cores, seeds. Shouldn't this sweetness
exist in the afterlife? I've heard that's what angels
crave those times they're glimpsed, partly visible,
a rustle of wings, an opening in the air. Apparently,
they shimmer, made of gossamer and light.
We always long for what we don't have,
and they yearn to be incarnate, to know the hunger
of the tongue. Filaments of cotton candy, fistfuls
of sugar, the long slow drip of honey and molasses.
I tried to sweeten my mother's last days, bringing
her a deconstructed sundae—coffee ice cream
in one cup, hot fudge in another, whipped cream
in a third. But her hunger is not appeased. She still
longs for this world, its confectionary
splendor. She would, if she could, open her mouth
like a bird or a baby, and let me spoon it in.

Deauville, le Paddock

after a painting by Raoul Dufy

This house, pink stucco, could be made of meringue,
a confection beaten out of egg white and light. If I bit
into it, sugar would melt on my tongue. Sunlight
drops like coins through the leaves of the plane trees;
a short lick of black defines every shadow. Behind it,
sky meets sea, rises, a field of cobalt. I imagine
our hearts to be pink as this house, moving blood
through delicate machinery, red on one side, blue
on the other. There's a riderless horse in one corner
of the picture, you've just alighted and are looking
into my eyes as if nothing in the world was as important
as what I might say next. I want to paint your body
with the pink sable of my tongue. I want to memorize
your skin. I want this blue afternoon to never end.

Rendezvous at Annecy

The lake is so blue, it colors the air,
makes you feel as if you're in an aquarium,
floating instead of walking, tucked inside
the scalloped Alps, a ladle full of sky—
And we are lucky to be here, and we know it,
another difficult year of loss, needless war,
peace broken like a baguette on the cobblestones,
crumbs to be squabbled over by pigeons and doves.
But, love, we are here, remembering Delacroix, how
the crust of the ordinary must be broken through,
the life where we don't have time to talk, but leave
notes on the place mats, where we wave as our cars
pass going up and down the hill.

Here, time is a gift to be slowly unwrapped,
like last night, when I took off your shirt,
and you slipped the shawl from my shoulders,
pulled me down on the cool smooth sheets.
In the morning, roses flushed the air pink,
and we lingered over coffee at the wrought iron table.
The language of the body, its many tongues.
The lake, lapping at the shore. The hive of the everyday
drones on the other side of the world, waiting.
But we are humming, our bodies' new translation,
accents—*circonflexe, grave,* and *aigue*—
like tattoos on our arms and legs.

Aubade

O, this morning, not a cloud in the sky, and coffee,
black, the way I like it. I have been watching a phoebe,
dark hood and wagtail bobbing, as he flits back and forth
from the beauty bush to the eave of the shed, just yards
from this red Adirondack chair where I'm sitting,
breathing the day through my skin. It rained last night,
and the chair's damp slats are cool on my back; there's
a scree of frogs in the swamp, a creek of sound
in the background, a river of desire: *Here I am. Find me.*
Felicitous. That's the only word to describe this. The sun
pours warm honey from its flask, no matter how little
we deserve it. Some of us drag a heavy load
through the day, a sack of should-ofs, or push a bushel
of sorrow up a hill. But there's the phoebe coming back
with his bit of straw or broken twig. He has a job to do,
and he sticks with it. And then he opens his beak and sings.

Weather Report

All this time on the planet, and still I am no wiser
than I was thirty years ago when I began to write,
scratching on a yellow pad while the voices in my head
screeched *not good enough*. They're still shrieking
their shrill words in my left ear, just above the migraine
that's singing a high E sharp from its perch in my brain.
Not good enough, and I know it, but today the sky
is that low blue note that comes after a storm,
and the locust is sending out round green messages
as it bobs and weaves in the wind. There's a flock
of cedar waxwings in the sumac, wearing
their little black masks, stealing the afternoon away.
The light streams in from the west, still I wrestle
with my old friends faith and doubt. A thin scribble
of clouds floats by, obscuring the sky, and all the words
are hiding, elusive as that bird over there, the one
that's singing its heart out, just out of sight.

Very Long Afternoons

Those were the long afternoons when poetry left me.
(Adam Zagajewski, "Long Afternoons")

Today, the sky's a bowl of blue, stippled by high
cirrus clouds that the wind has combed through,
and the air is full of roses and birdsong.
But I'm having a black dog Franz Wright
I Hate Myself and Want to Die Day, at a well-bottom
loss for words. *Literature will lose, sunlight will win,*
don't worry, he wrote, and sure enough, there's the sun,
ahead by a furlong, hurtling down the hardpacked track,
hoofbeats a roll of muffled thunder. I'm late
out of the gate, plodding in the back. Everyone else,
writers with books, the hot new MFAs, is in a lather,
speeding down the backstretch and into the money,
dreaming of black-eyed Susans. I'm trying to write
a line or two, or maybe just an image. The soft breeze
is full of peonies, iris, as if some baker had sugared
the air, and the late afternoon sun glazes everything
golden. Wake me when it's over, this life.

Judas Tree

. . . the one destined to be lost,
so that the scripture might be fulfilled. John 17:12

Driving south to Virginia, what catches the eye, stays
the heart, are the redbud trees, oddly named because
they're not red at all, but purple, the pluperfect of purple,
their baubled beads lining the thin wands of their limbs
in a winy haze. They're also called Judas trees;
according to legend, it's the tree he hanged
himself on, once strong enough to bear a man's body,
now weak and spindly in shame. The flowers, too,
are abashed, blushing magenta instead of white.
But I've never understood the bad rap on Judas;
without him, the story's not complete. Don't we sing
Prepare the royal highway? Don't these trees line
the roadsides waving their psalms like palms?
Wasn't our favorite drink in college the Purple Jesus,
grape Kool-Aid and vodka? And doesn't this tree
wear its heart on its sleeve, flushing out each May
in ventricular pale green leaves?

God's Tears

after "Guidebook," by Claire Giblin,
ink and acrylic on Yupo

The petals open like silk umbrellas, the tiny stamens
bearing God's tears. The way mine bloomed
this morning, reading the news that you were gone,
halfway around the world in Dingle by the sea.
Back home, we grow fuchsias in pots, lose them
as soon as frost comes, but here, they tower over
my head, form thick hedges that line the narrow
roads, a tunnel of scarlet. You were both
salty and sweet, difficult and a good friend.
You would have loved these Wexford strawberries
in September, even while you'd have scoffed
at the thought of growing them this far north.
The hedgerows move with the wind's song:
fluttering ballerinas in crimson skirts,
purple petticoats, long long legs;
their tiny toes pointing toward earth.

The Burren

ań bhoireann, a rocky place

We walked down the gravelly path, limestone
karst on either side, to see the wedge grave,
a megalith four thousand years old,
both burial and worship site. But it
was roped off with warning signs,
and we were in a field of tourists,
the languages of Babel filling the air.
No space for awe wedged in there.
In a nearby linden tree, a robin redbreast
sang through his throat, his beak as closed
as the secrets of the dolmen. Back
in the parking lot, a dark-haired girl
was selling earrings and pendants
made from local clay, carved
with Celtic designs: knot, triquetra,
triskalon, triple spiral. I felt like I knew
her, she looked like my friend Clare,
fifty years younger. Clare, who told me,
*You have to see the Burren, it's like nothing
else on earth.* Clare, whose liver was failing,
whose health I prayed for daily. What I didn't know
then was that the rest of her life had cracked apart
like this limestone shield, her lawyer son in jail
for embezzling, awaiting trial. Now all she could
think of was tucking him in at night, wondering
if he had a blanket, wondering if he was cold,
knowing the harm he'd done, that his brothers
and sisters had disowned him. But in this rocky
place, here she is, young again, her face unlined,
her hair unwired with silver, her six children
unborn. Here, in this field of stones,
without machines, somehow humans raised up

these huge table stones, then lifted the massive
slant roof slab. And prayed to the wild stars
that it would hold.

Stones

after "Jade Mountain I and II," by Claire Giblin,
acrylic and ink on Yupo

Sometimes, our journeys take us off the maps. Like when
we were in Dingle, and stumbled on the Famine Cottages,
not mentioned in any guidebook, nor starred on the circuit
map though every other pile of old stones, from
the 2500-year-old ring fort to the ruined churches
to the stone beehives, called *clocháns*, are clearly marked.
An Gortá Mór, the great famine, tragedy not just because
most West Kerry families lived on potatoes and a bit
of milk, but because the English landlords had hearts
like a cairn of stones, refused to send relief. Yet
Muckross House had three hundred sixty-five windows,
one for each day of the year. A million died, a million
more went west over the sea, never to return. Fishermen
sold their nets to pay rent, while the ocean, teeming
with fish, glistened and gleamed. Yes, there were cattle,
and fields gold with ripening wheat, all of which went
to England to be sold. The sky closed like an oyster shell
over their heads. Towards the end, when the suffering
could no longer be denied, food bundles were given
only to those families that worked the Hunger Roads.
Men in rags, walking skeletons, died where they dropped,
in the shingle. And there the roads stopped, too.

Salt

On the boulevard, the Bradford pears
release their petals; they spill like salt
on the ground. My grandmother would
have pinched up the granules, thrown them over
her shoulder to fool the evil eye. My mother
would have said *Don't cry over what's spilled*.
When we were in Brittany, we saw *les artisan
paludiers* harvest it by hand, marketed as *fleur de sel*.
When we poured my mother's ashes in the ocean,
they ran through my hands like grains from a silver
spout. On the blue canister in my kitchen, there's
a little girl standing in the rain in a yellow dress,
the same can of salt under her arm, open, running out,
like those Dutch interiors repeating themselves
in convex mirrors, repeating like the bits of DNA
in molecules that become the coins in our ovaries' purse,
doled out month by month, drawn by the moon. Long ago,
someone tipped some salt on a black skillet,
and decided to call that spillage "stars."

Pistachios

They're already half-cracked, aren't they,
the smooth shells swinging open, the tongue
of the nut peeping out. I stare at the one
in my hand, and I'm back at the museum
in Vancouver, where there's a sculpture
of First Man curled in a clam shell, Raven
perched on top, waiting for it to crack open,
for Humans to be born. If I had known then
how much sorrow lay ahead, was yet to be borne,
could I have let my heart open like that? This shell
unfolds like some strange green flower to the sun.
It's no accident that things newly minted are green,
that the grass springs up green when April comes
round again. Though some think being green
means unformed, unripe, even envy
is jealous of green, its freshness, its hope. The sun,
at day's end, loves slipping behind the horizon,
sometimes flashing green. The way this small nut
slips perfectly back into its shell, although you
can never quite click the lid, tuck in the world's
sorrows, make it stick tight, once the hinge
is broken, and the crack that's in everything
has let the light back in.

Zucchini

So, now we're at the end of the line,
a row of zeros, the 26th step
of a long straight ladder; *finito,*
basta, the last stroke, the slash
of Zorro's sword . . . .

And here we find you, deep
in the heart of the garden
at the zenith of summer,
green Zeppelins floating
in a scratchy-leaved sky. . . .

Although you start small
from an oval tear-shaped
seed, quickly there's a sprout,
then two heart-shaped leaves,
and suddenly, you've taken
over the whole garden, nudged
out the radishes, covered up
the beans, hogged all the sunlight,
growing faster than I can say
ratatouille three times . . . .

In Corsica, my ancestors weeded
around your roots with *zappas,*
leaned on them to survey their *zolas,*
small plots, hoed them smooth
as a Zamboni clears the ice . . . .

We serve you up stuffed and broiled
with cheese topping, shredded
in quick bread with raisins and walnuts,
sautéed with tarragon, stewed with tomatoes
and basil, stir-fried in olive oil,
or in a cold *zuppa*, sour cream
floating on top. We even nibble
your flowers, dipped in batter, golden-fried.

Then, at summer's end, we find
what's left, lurking in the leaves:
an enormous baseball bat flung
in the corner, abandoned, waiting
patiently for the seasons to whirl
around again, bringing the start
of spring training, the sun, ascending
like the letter A, rosy in the east.

Notes

Goddesses is dedicated to Pat Valdata.

A Woman Is Her Mother. That's the Main Thing is a semi-glosa (invented, or nonce form). The title is a line by Anne Sexton, and the italicized lines are by Dylan Thomas and Sharon Olds.

At the Observatory in Sweet Briar, Under a Field of Stars is dedicated to Katharyn Levy, Tom Doran, and Lisa Weil.

At VCCA, I Hear a Red-Bellied Woodpecker, and Think of Martha Silano, VCCA stands for the Virginia Center for the Creative Arts, an artist colony and a wonderful place to live and work. Martha Silano is a Seattle poet who I met there in 2000.

Intro to Lit is dedicated to Gail Price.

Willow Ware
"Volare" was a popular song recorded in the 1950s by Domenico Modugno. "Nel blu dipinto di blu" translates as "in the blue painted blue."

Rendezvous at Annecy
The opening lines were suggested by a letter of Zelda Fitzgerald's.

Very Long Afternoons
Franz Wright is a Pulitzer Prize winning poet who addresses subjects of isolation, illness, spirituality and gratitude.

God's Tears is dedicated to the memory of Adrianne Marcus.
Deora Dé, another name for wild fuchsia, means God's tears in Irish.

The Burren is dedicated to the memory of Clare Reidy.

Pistachios
The last two lines reference a song by Leonard Cohen.

Made in the USA
Middletown, DE
10 November 2019